An Educational
Read and Color
Book of
CALIFORNIA
MISSIONS

CONTENTS

EDITOR
Linda Spizzirri

ILLUSTRATION
Peter M. Spizzirri

COVER ART
Peter M. Spizzirri

This Is An Educational Coloring Book of CALIFORNIA MISSIONS • Published by SPIZZIRRI PUBLISHING, INC., P.O. BOX 9397, RAPID CITY, SOUTH DAKOTA 57709. No part of this publication may be reproduced by any means without the express written consent of the publisher. All national and international rights reserved on the entire contents of this publication. Printed in U.S.A.

In our civilized world, it is almost impossible to imagine what it must have been like over 200 years ago along the California coast. There were no cities, no freeways, no airplanes to quickly go over the mountains, no electricity, etc. There were only huge uncharted areas of wilderness. Travel was difficult, dangerous, and slow.

The idea of mission establishment had been a successful one for Spain. By moving into Alta California, with the purpose of converting and educating the natives, both the Catholic Church and Spain's possessions would grow. The long range plan was to give the mission complex, its land, stock, crops, and its total operation over to the trained Indians who lived there, within a 10 year period. The Church would simply maintain possession of the church and padres' quarters at each mission site. The transition from church to independent owners is a process called secularization. Besides increasing her territories, Spain also wanted to stop any southern advancement by Russia.

With plans to establish the first three California missions, three ships set sail from La Paz (on the Baja California peninsula), for San Diego in 1769. An overland party, led by Fr. Junipero Serra, had left weeks earlier from Loreto, Mexico. The sea party suffered through Pacific storms, scurvy, and the loss of one ship. The overland journey through the Baja desert, the wilderness, and hostile Indians took a heavy toll on the land travelers. When the two parties met at San Diego Bay, there were very few survivors, and many of them were sick. The first mission was established at San Diego, as planned, even though there was a lack of men and supplies needed to make the mission a success. The Indians in the area were hostile and unwilling to accept the soldiers and the missionaries. The Indian tribes were not as civilized as the Spanish had expected, so converting and training them was a difficult task.

The missions were built in a standard quadrangle shape. The church was the most important building in the quadrangle. Many churches had a false front, called an espadaña. It was commonly used on Spanish buildings to make them seem larger than if the true, low roofline were showing. Another typical Spanish feature was the campanario, which is not a bell steeple, but simply a wall with holes pierced in it for the bells to be placed. The corredor, an outdoor hallway with open arches, was a typical Spanish feature that was often used along the inner walls of the quadrangle. The other buildings of the quadrangle were divided into needed living quarters, storage rooms, and workshops. Houses for the Indians that lived and worked at the mission were erected outside the quadrangle. All buildings were simple and serviceable. Design and decoration was usually limited to the church.

From a slow beginning, the missions grew, prospered, and spread into a chain of 21 missions that spread from San Diego to San Francisco. The missions produced huge crops and maintained large herds. Unfortunately, the Indians of the California missions were not prepared to manage when secularization was forced upon them. Spain was no longer in charge. Mexico declared its independence and a declining Spanish empire was unable to stop her. When Mexico took control it was hard to tell who was in charge because Governors came and went rapidly. No longer under the padres control, land speculators were able to get the mission lands. The missions quickly fell from civilized prosperous settlements, into ruin. After the United States took California from Mexico, most of the missions were returned to the Church by Acts of Congress, along with the lands of the original quadrangle. All the 21 missions have been at least partially restored, and a few plan full restoration of the complete original quadrangle. All are special and worth visiting. The missions illustrated in this book are pictured as they appear today. Enjoy your pictorial journey through this book.

WHERE TO FIND THE CALIFORNIA MISSIONS

Mission	Name	Founded
1st	San Diego de Alcalá	1769
2nd	San Carlos Borromeo de Carmelo	1770
3rd	San Antonio de Padua	1771
4th	San Gabriel Arcángel	1771
5th	San Luis Obispo de Tolosa	1772
6th	San Francisco de Asís	1776
7th	San Juan Capistrano	1776
8th	Santa Clara de Asís	1777
9th	San Buenaventura	1782
10th	Santa Bárbara	1786
11th	La Purísima Concepción	1787
12th	Santa Cruz	1791
13th	Nuestra Señora de la Soledad	1791
14th	San José	1797
15th	San Juan Bautista	1797
16th	San Miguel Arcángel	1797
17th	San Fernando Rey de España	1797
18th	San Luis Rey de Francia	1798
19th	Santa Inés	1804
20th	San Rafael Arcángel	1817
21st	San Francisco Solano	1823

CALIFORNIA

San Francisco Solano
San Rafael Arcángel

SAN FRANCISCO
San Francisco de Asís
San José
Santa Clara de Asís
Santa Cruz
San Juan Bautista
San Carlos Borromeo de Carmelo
Nuestra Señora de la Soledad
San Antonio de Padua
San Miguel Arcángel
San Luis Obispo de Tolosa
Santa Inés
La Purísima Concepción
Santa Bárbara
San Buenaventura
San Fernando Rey de España
San Gabriel Arcángel
LOS ANGELES
San Juan Capistrano
San Luis Rey de Francia
San Diego de Alcalá
SAN DIEGO

N

El Camino Real" was the connecting path between all 21 missions. The foot path became the stage
ute and, with very few changes, is Highway 101 today. It still is often referred to as El Camino Real.

San Diego de Alcalá

A tall brick cross on a hill overlooking San Diego Bay marks the site of the first mission, dedicated by Fr. Serra in July of 1769. The Spanish had carefully worked out plans for the establishment of three missions: San Diego in Southern California, Monterey in the North to stop any southern advancement by Russia, and a third to be midway to span the great distance between these two points. The settlers at San Diego could do little but erect crude shelters, because they were so sick after the long journey from Mexico. Conditions were so bad, if a supply ship had not arrived, the mission party would have been ordered back to New Spain. The Indians around the mission were unhappy about the invasion of these new people and their new ways. They were not interested in being converted to Christianity. In time, Fr. Serra was able to baptize and convert some Indians to his mission. The original site chosen for the mission was abandoned in 1774, and a new site was chosen 6 miles up the river. In 1776, in an effort to stop the expansion of Christianity, hostile Indians banded together in a night raid to rid themselves of the intruders. They set fire to the mission, but failed to force the Spanish to leave. Such a raid on a mission never occurred again and all future missions were established with military protection. The San Diego mission was reconstructed in a full quadrangle, to protect it like a military fort. The small adobe church was dedicated in 1813. When restoration of California's first mission started in 1931, only the facade of the little adobe church was still standing. The small church, restored in its stark simplicity, with its bell tower and beautiful gardens is located in San Diego's Mission Valley, 5 miles east of Highway 5.

San Carlos Borromeo de Carmelo

In 1770, Fr. Serra left San Diego and went north to Monterey to establish his second mission, as planned. He selected a site near the presidio (soldier's quarters), but this proved to be a mistake. The Indians were uncomfortable so close to the Spanish soldiers. In addition, conditions were not good for producing the crops that were so necessary for the mission to survive. Fr. Serra moved his mission to a new site in the beautiful Carmel Valley. He used the Carmel location as headquarters for the entire chain of missions that were to develop. A wooden chapel and the needed buildings were erected in 6 months, but Fr. Serra's dream was to have a beautiful stone church. In 1791, a stone mason was imported for the task. The cornerstone was laid in 1793 and four years later the stone church was dedicated on the same site as the wooden church. After secularization, the church fell to ruin. The roof collapsed in 1851 and the walls stood unprotected from the elements until 1881 when funds were raised to put a shingled roof on the structure. The new roof did not improve the appearance very much, but it did serve the purpose of protecting the church from total ruin. Harry Downie has supervised the restoration of the mission to its present state. Considered to be the most beautiful of the California missions, it boasts a beautiful mountain and sea setting, sandstone walls, Moorish towers, and the famous striking star window above the arched doorway of the front entrance, with its huge hand carved doors. The Carmel site also boasts complete restoration of a mission quadrangle rather than just the church restoration.

San Antonio de Padua

San Bonaventura was originally planned to be the third California mission. When unsettled conditions postponed its founding, the impatient Fr. Serra simply directed his efforts to an alternate mission. In a remote Valley of the Oaks, the San Antonia de Padua mission was established in July of 1771. It became known for its huge crops of wheat, which were processed into flour using a large water powered gristmill. The now famous clay tiles were first used on the modest chapel at San Antonio. The original facade of the chapel was probably very plain. It is not known exactly when the elegant companario that is unique to this mission was added. After secularization the mission fell into such total ruin, that when it was offered for sale in 1845, not one person placed a bid to buy it. Luckily the California Historic Landmarks League and the Native Sons of California selected San Antonio mission (not just the church) for restoration. Restoration was started in 1903 and the church was restored by 1907. In 1948 it was decided that to do proper restoration, all buildings but the church would be leveled. Because the restoration was done so carefully we now have a mission that duplicates the 1813 original in approximate size and atmosphere. The mission compound is located 23 miles southwest of King City (off Highway 101).

San Gabriel Arcángel

The fourth mission, which was founded in 1771 by Frs. Cambon and Somera, was a primitive structure that progressed little due to the lack of converts (attributed to acts of the cruel soldiers) and crop failure. In 1775 a new site was chosen and construction began on a second structure. The mission began to prosper. The fertile valley produced fine crops, large herds, and a magnificent vineyard that produced as much as 50,000 gallons of wine a year. It took twenty-six years to complete the new church that was started in 1779. Unique among the mission churches, it had long narrow windows and capped buttresses, a style copying a cathedral in Cordova, Spain. Secularization hit hard at San Gabriel, but the church has survived unchanged. The mission church and its beautiful gardens are located on Mission Drive in San Gabriel and are under the protection of the Claretian Fathers.

San Luis Obispo de Tolosa

Fr. Serra was on his way to Monterey Bay in 1772, when he stopped near the Valley of the Bears. On a small hill near a stream, he selected a location for the San Luis Obispo Mission. The fifth mission grew slowly. The mission constantly suffered damage from the burning arrows of Indian attacks. The dry tule (large bulrushes common in California) roofs burned quickly. This led to the development of the now famous curved tiles for the roof. Manufacturing was started in 1790, first used for all the buildings at San Luis Obispo, and then the other missions as they were built. The church remained in its original state until the late 1870's when roof tiles were removed and the face was boarded up. The whole front was taken down and a New England style bell steeple was built. The inside was also changed drastically. Fortunately, restoration in 1947 returned both the interior and exterior to its original state. The mission colonnade is unique with its square openings and round pillars. It is located in downtown San Luis Obispo, on the corner of Monterey and Chorro Streets.

San Francisco de Asís

In 1776, Fr. Francisco Palóu selected a site on the huge northern bay (San Francisco Bay) to erect the sixth mission in the mission chain. The first simple chapel was a wooden structure plastered with mud. It is commonly called Mission Dolores, getting its name from the little stream and nearby lake. Mission Dolores had constant problems with labor. The Indian helpers ran away because they enjoyed their freedom more than daily work. Its farming progress and production was hampered by sea winds and chilly fogs. A permanent church was started in 1782 and dedicated in 1791. This beautiful church and a tiny cemetery are all that is left of the original mission complex, but it remains as it was back in 1791. The small structure miraculously survived the earthquake and fire of 1906 and today is lovingly cared for as San Franciso's oldest building. Located at 16th & Dolores Streets in San Francisco, this popular little church has a simple exterior. The interior shows an extensive use of redwood and Indian design chevrons decorate the plain beam ceilings. Many examples of Indian art can still be seen at the mission today.

12

San Buenaventura

In 1782, San Buenaventura was the ninth and last mission founded by the famous Fr. Serra. It was completed under his capable successor, Fr. Lasuén. The numerous Indians in the area were friendly and intelligent. They lived in igloo-style houses and slept on beds with reed mattresses. As craftsmen, the Indians were famous for building huge pine-board canoes and their basketry, even weaving water tight baskets. The mission was prosperous, as expected, and produced bountiful harvests of not only the usual fruits and grains, but also exotic crops such as bananas, figs, and sugar cane. The original mission church was destroyed by fire and was replaced by a larger structure made of stone that took 15 years to build. All that is left of the original mission grounds is this little church that is completely engulfed by the town of Ventura. It remains much as it was in 1809, except that after the earthquake of 1812, when repairs were made, huge buttresses were added to protect the historic church from future tremor damage.

San Juan Capistrano

The mission site was chosen the first time by Fr. Serra in 1776, but he returned to San Diego because of Indian trouble. Fr. Lasuén returned to the site one year later (1777) and started construction of the seventh mission. In its prime, this mission was, by far, the most prosperous. It had bountiful crops and 20,000 cattle and sheep. In 1796 construction was begun on a new large stone church. A master stone mason was brought from Mexico and put in charge of the construction. The hard working Indians brought sandstone, in a never ending procession, from six miles away. It took nine years to build the magnificent cathedral-like church. It was 180 feet long and 40 feet wide, seven domes surmounted the vaulted ceiling, and a 120 foot bell tower crowned the main entrance. When all of California celebrated its completion in 1806, no one thought that this magnificent structure would last only nine years. In December of 1812, an earthquake destroyed all but the sanctuary of the church and killed 40 praying Indians in the falling rubble. Such a project as rebuilding of the huge church was never considered. Services were returned to the small adobe chapel that is referred to as "Fr. Serra's Church". With secularization, came the neglect of the mission buildings that caused them to fall into ruin. The use of dynamite in 1860, during an attempted restoration of the stone church, caused even more damage. In 1890, restorers were able to save the original Serra Church. The latest restoration was begun in 1920 by Fr. St. John O'Sullivan, who also planted the gardens that make the mission such a romantic site. Migration of the swallows returning to Capistrano every St. Joseph's day (March 19) has made the name of this mission a household word. It is located on Highway 5, just off hwy 101.

Santa Clara de Asís

The cross that was erected to mark the second San Francisco Bay mission, in 1777, still stands in a protective redwood covering, in front of the present Santa Clara mission church. The eighth mission was founded with the hope that two missions might better protect the "Great Northern Bay" from any enemy attack or occupation of this strategic point. The mission prospered because of the fertile land and because the Indian artisans became known for their weaving. Natural disasters of fire, flood, and earthquake plagued the mission. By 1781 an adobe church was started after a series of floods damaged many mission buildings and destroyed the first two log churches. By 1825 the church was rebuilt for the fifth time. In an effort to please the people of the newly established town of San Jose, Indians planted rows of black willows to grace the road (Alameda) from the mission to the settlement. Santa Clara was one of the last missions to be secularized, but the lands were quickly dispersed. When the lands were partly returned to the Church, after American occupation, the Church was given to the Jesuits to use as a seat for California's college. The church, which was remodeled in 1861 and 1887, was completely destroyed by a fire in 1926. The church that stands on the Santa Clara campus today is a stucco and concrete model of the 1825 original. One large bell, that was given to the mission by the King of Spain in 1798, survived the fire and can still be heard ringing every evening.

Santa Bárbara

Fr. Serra died before he could start the beautiful Santa Bárbara mission of his dreams. The capable Fr. Lasuén, his successor, founded the tenth mission, in 1786. The sophisticated water system that was built around the mission was constructed so well that parts of it are in existence today. By 1812, the church had been enlarged four different times to accommodate the growing mission. After the earthquake of 1812, the nearly destroyed church was repaired and used until a great stone church could be built. Highly trained Chumash Indian craftsmen constructed the new Church under the direction of padre Antonio Ripall. He used a Spanish translation of a six-volume set of books on Roman architecture. The unique Roman and Spanish style church was completed in 1820 and boasts the only twin bell towers in the mission chain. The church that is standing today is the same church. An earthquake in 1925 damaged the facade, towers, and a wing of the mission. The church was totally restored but in 1950 cracks appeared in the facade. The front was completely dismantled and rebuilt with steel reinforced concrete, but retained the dimensions and appearance of the original church. This magnificent "Queen of the Missions" never suffered the ruin that so many of the missions did. Secularization proved disastrous for the Indians who lived here, but not for the church itself. It always remained in the possession of the Catholic Church; first as an Indian mission, then as a parish church for white settlers. Besides the restored parts of the old mission, a museum, and historic church, the Santa Bárbara Mission also houses the seminary for the Franciscan priesthood. Any new construction follows the foundation lines of the old mission quadrangle and the new building designs are kept in harmony with the original buildings. The complex is located at 2201 Laguna Drive in Santa Bárbara.

La Purísima Concepción

Fr. Lasuén established the eleventh mission halfway between San Luis Obispo and Santa Bárbara, in 1787. The mission buildings were poorly constructed during the first year and quickly disintegrated. New buildings were completed by 1802. In 1812, two earthquakes and a flood totally destroyed the mission. The mission had enjoyed such success for 24 years, it didn't seem possible such total devastation could be unleashed by mother nature. The padres rebuilt the mission 4 1/2 miles from the original site. It is the only mission that was built in a straight line instead of the standard quadrangle. As one of the most completely restored missions, it enables visitors to see how the padres and their Indian helpers lived, and the tools they used for work. The mission is located 5 miles east of Lompoc, and is part of a 500 acre state historic site.

Santa Cruz

In 1791, Fr. Lasuén founded the twelfth mission in such a perfect location that the mission should have been very successful. However, amiable Indians, good climate and fertile soil were no match for the evil influences brought to the mission by hostile and immoral people that established a pueblo (town) very close by. The towns' people illegally settled on mission land, taking what they wanted of its stock, crops and possessions. The mission never prospered and, at its peak, its converts numbered the lowest of any mission. It was the first mission to be secularized and rapidly fell into ruin. In 1857, an earthquake demolished whatever remained standing of the church. In 1931, with no pretense of duplicating style or size, a small memorial church was erected 200 feet from the original church site. A two-story portion of the soldiers' barracks stands close by, which is the only structure remaining from the early mission period. It is located at Emmet & School Streets, Santa Cruz.

Nuestra Señora de la Soledad

Soledad is the Spanish word for loneliness. The thirteenth mission, founded in 1791 by Fr. Lasuén, was properly named. The desolate spot in the Salinas River Valley was so lonely, the padres that were sent to the mission constantly requested transfers from the inclement valley. Both the building of the mission complex and conversion of the Indians was a slow process. It was six years before a permanent church was finished. The mission did prosper after the padres developed an irrigation system to bring water from the nearby Salinas River to the rich bottom land. Good crops and large herds brought success to the mission. Unfortunately, the very river that brought life to the mission, also destroyed it. A series of floods from 1824 to 1832 brought life at the mission complex to an end. By the time restoration of the mission was started in 1954, only a front corner of the original chapel structure remained. After extensive restoration, the mission looks today as it did in 1820. It is part of the parish of Soledad and is located 3 miles south of town.

San José

When Fr. Lasuén founded the San José Mission in the summer of 1797, he realized it would be located in a hostile area. The Indians were anything but eager to give up their way of life. From a very slow start, of only 33 converts the first year, the mission grew and eventually claimed more converts than any other northern mission. It also led in the production of crops such as wheat, corn, and beans. This inland mission, fourteenth in the chain, served as a major military base throughout most of its existence. The large plain adobe church which was erected to house its many converts (6,737 in 39 years), was completely destroyed by an earthquake in 1868. This rebuilt structure that is illustrated, was part of the original monastery. It is only a small part of what once was a large mission complex. Today it only serves as a museum and chapel. It is located 15 miles northeast of San José.

San Juan Bautista

San Juan Bautista is the fifteenth mission in the twenty-one mission chain, and one of the four founded in the summer of 1797 by the energetic Fr. Lasuén. The little mission grew quickly and by 1803 construction was started on a large permanent church. Consideration was given to a unique three aisle church, but a series of earthquakes convinced the padres to fill in the open arches and to construct the church as a standard single aisle mission church. This proved to be a wise decision. Even though this church was erected right on the great San Andreas fault, it survived the large earthquakes of 1812 and 1906 that destroyed so many of the other missions in the chain. The colors on the inside of the church are just as bright as when they were painted in 1818. The church, located in the town of San Juan Bautista, has been in use since its completion. A part of the original El Camino Real going past the mission, the unchanged mission church, and a series of buildings preserved as state historical monuments contribute to a sense of being able to step back in time to the early mission days.

24

San Miguel Arcángel

Fr. Lasuén erected a mud roofed church, in 1797, to establish the sixteenth mission and thereby shorten the long distance between the San Antonio and San Luis Obispo missions. In one year a larger church had to be erected. This church lasted until 1806 when a fire destroyed many of the mission buildings and all of the supplies that the Indians and padres so badly needed. This unfortunate incident led to the careful planning of a tile-roofed permanent church. The Spanish artist, Estévan Munras, was imported to decorate the interior of the church. To step into this church is to take a step back in time. Earthquakes, passage of time, and vandals that destroyed so many of the other missions, have miraculously left this church untouched. Even those in charge of restoration have resisted the temptation to change or in any way retouch the paintings of Munras, so this little church remains exactly as it was in 1806! This mission, with its unusual colonnade of 16 arches of different shapes and sizes, is located 9 miles north of Paso Robles.

San Luis Rey de Francia

Twenty years after the Spanish first encountered the friendly Indians in this area, Fr. Lasuén founded his ninth and last mission. In June of 1798, he founded the eighteenth mission in the chain and baptized 54 babies. The immediate acceptance of the mission by the Indians contributed to the immediate success of the "King of the Missions." Construction began immediately and was in continuous progress throughout the life of the mission. During the first year the necessary buildings were erected and in the next two years the structures were roofed with kiln dried tiles. Soon construction on the permanent church began and took ten years to complete. Only this church and the one at Capistrano (demolished in an earthquake) were constructed in this cruciform design. The quadrangle of this mission covered a six acre area and the huge white structure was described as, "looking like a palace." At the point of secularization, the converts numbered about 3,000 and its impressive herds numbered almost 60,000 head of livestock. The mission was saved from ruin by the Franciscans who started restoration in 1893. Because the mission was to become a seminary, much attention was given to its restoration, and it is hoped in time it will become a completely restored quadrangle. The beautifully restored church is much as it was when the padres and early Christians worshipped here. Inside the quadrangle stands a huge pepper tree, the first brought to California. The mission is located in the town of San Luis Rey, off Highway 76.

San Fernando Rey de España

Because of the traveling distance from San Buenaventura on the coast to San Gabriel in the interior, Fr. Lasuén decided to establish a new mission midway between them. He chose for his site a location among friendly Indians and flowing streams. The seventeenth mission, San Fernando Rey de España was founded in 1797. A small chapel was erected immediately, but a larger church had to be built within a year. The number of converts grew to 1,000, and in 1806 an even larger adobe mission church was finished. The church barely survived the earthquake of 1812, and over a period of time it completely collapsed. The huge Mission House, which measured 243 feet long and 50 feet wide, has withstood the test of time. Even though the building was used at its low point in time (1896) as a hog farm, the original structure still stands. Crops from the mission were bountiful, but the most important industry was cattle raising. At one time it boasted a herd of up to 22,000 head of cattle. This mission, which is located 1 1/2 miles west of San Fernando on Mission Blvd., is still being restored at this time.

Santa Inés

The lovely Santa Inés Valley was the secluded setting for the nineteenth mission, which was founded in 1804 by Fr. Estévan Tápis. Eight years of building was barely completed when the great earthquake of 1812 destroyed the church and damaged many buildings. The rebuilt church was dedicated in 1817. Santa Inés quickly became famous for its rich crops and large herds, which numbered up to 13,000 animals. The mission prospered until the Indian Revolt of 1824. Peace was restored between the Indians and the soldiers, but the mission never returned to its previous prosperity. The mission was never vacant, but fell into disrepair. In 1904, Fr. Alexander Buckler started a 20 year restoration project. You can get an idea as to the size of the original mission, if you realize that the restored buildings are about one fourth of the original mission quadrangle. This mission, which is the favorite of many people, is located at 1760 Mission Drive in Solvang.

San Rafael Arcángel

The fog and dampness of San Francisco caused much illness among the Indians at Mission Dolores. It was decided that a branch mission across the bay would be erected to serve as a hospital. This branch was built on the sunny side of the bay in 1817, under the direction of Fr. Vicente de Sarría. Under the warm sun and the capable healing hands of Fr. Gil (a padre knowledgeable in medicine), the branch hospital became successful and widely known. The little hospital was given full mission status in 1823, making it the twentieth mission in the chain. The usual quadrangle was never completed here. Only a simple chapel was erected at a right angle to an 87 foot long building that was divided for storehouses, hospital, and monastery. Instead of the usual bell tower, the bells were simply hung on a cross beam in front of the little chapel. San Rafael reached its potential as a mission and a hospital in 1823, was abandoned in 1842, and was torn down in 1890. It was not until recently that a replica of the mission was constructed near its original site, 15 miles north of San Francisco in San Rafael.

San Francisco Solano

The twenty-first, the last, and the most northern of the missions was founded in 1823 by the ambitious Fr. José Altimira. The padre was so unpopular that the Indian converts either ran away or were part of a band that rebelled by looting and burning the mission in 1826, thus driving out the unkind Fr. Altimira. His replacement, Fr. Fortuni, worked for seven years to bring the mission back to its original strength. The wood and thatch buildings were replaced with adobe and a new larger adobe church was built in 1827. When Fr. Fortuni retired, there were thirty structures to the mission complex. As with all of the missions, with secularization came the decline of this mission. The church was kept in repair for a time but eventually fell into ruin. A new smaller adobe church was built in 1841, on the site where Fr. Altimira built the first small wooden church. In 1903 the Historic Landmarks League purchased the mission site. In 1911-12 and 1943-44 the mission church was repaired and restored. It is located in Sonoma, 20 miles north of San Francisco.

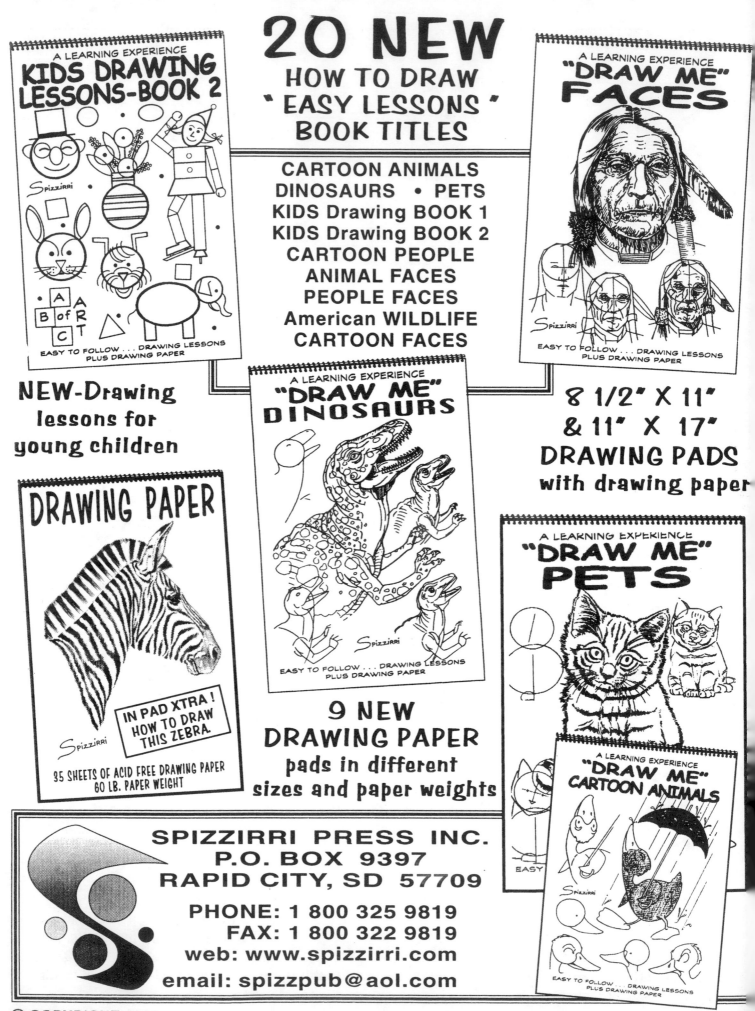